BELIAL

The
Wicked Ruler
Luke 10:19

BELIAL

The
Wicked Ruler

John Eckhardt

Crusaders Ministries
Chicago, Illinois

Unless otherwise indicated, all scriptural quotations are from the *King James Version* of the Bible.

BELIAL, The Wicked Ruler
ISBN 1-883927-08-0
Copyright © 1996, 1998
John Eckhardt
P.O. Box 7211
Chicago, Illinois 60680

Second printing
1st printing 1,500 copies

Editorial Consultant: Debra Marshall
Published by
Crusaders Ministries
P.O. Box 7211
Chicago, Illinois 60680
U.S.A.

Cover design and Book text production by
Dominion Marketing and Design Group
P.O. Box 609 Matteson, Illinois 60443-0609

Cover Illustration by: Donald Garner/Tommy Marcus Jr.

Printed in the United States of America.

Contents

Foreword

Spirits Under the Strongman of Belial

Scripture References For Belial

Appendix

Foreword

Then goeth he, and taketh with himself seven other spirits MORE WICKED THAN HIMSELF, and they enter in and dwell there: and the last state of that man is worse than the first. Even so shall it be unto this WICKED generation.

Matthew 12:45

Although all evil spirits are wicked, it is evident from this verse of Scripture that there are some spirits "more wicked" than others. According to the previous verse, there are also generations that are wicked because of the spirits that inhabit them.

Webster defines *wicked* as "morally very bad, evil, fierce, vicious, disposed to mischief, roguish, disgustingly unpleasant, vice, going beyond reasonable and predictable limits."

In other words, there are demons more fierce, vicious and vile than others. One of the most wicked and vile spirits in the kingdom of darkness is the *spirit of BELIAL.*

He is a *ruling* spirit of *wickedness.* There are a host of demons that operate under his command that we will discuss in this book. "Belial" is mentioned twenty-seven times in the Old Testament and once in the New Testament. It is from the Hebrew word *beliyaal* which is translated as *Belial* sixteen times in the Old Testament.

This word is also translated in other verses as *wicked, ungodly,* and *naughty.* The Strong's definition of *beliyaal* is "without profit, worthlessness, destruction, wickedness, evil, naughty." The most common of these definitions is *worthlessness.*

Webster's definition of *worthless* is "valueless, useless, contemptible, despicable", and *despicable* is defined as "deserving to be despised: so worthless or obnoxious as to rouse moral indignation."

Therefore, BELIAL'S WORK is to cause men to commit sins that are so vile and contemptible that it ROUSES MORAL INDIGNATION. All sin is wrong and I don't make any excuses or allowances for any sin. However, there are some sins more abominable than others. That is, there are different *degrees* of sin.

Under the law, there were some sins that were considered "abominations" and punishable by death, while other sins required certain sacrifices. Belial's work is to draw a nation into such abominable sins that it will bring the curse and the judgment of God.

When I observe the practices and sins that are happening in our nation, I know that the spirit of Belial is behind them. Belial is a strongman in America as well as other nations of the world. Belial is a world ruler of wickedness. Jesus taught us the necessity of binding the strongman in order to spoil his goods (Matthew 12:29). As previously stated, this strongman has a list of demons at his disposal that he has released upon our society.

Chapter 1
BELIAL AND
THE SPIRIT OF IDOLATRY

If thou shalt hear say in one of thy cities, which the Lord thy God hath given thee to dwell there, saying,

Certain men, the children of Belial, are gone out from among you, and have withdrawn the inhabitants of their city, saying, Let us go and serve other gods, which ye have not known;

Then shalt thou enquire, and make search, and ask diligently; and, behold, if it be truth, and the thing certain, that such abomination is wrought among you;

Thou shalt surely smite the inhabitants of that city with the edge of the sword, destroying it utterly, and all that is therein, and the cattle thereof, with the edge of the sword.

And thou shalt gather all the spoil of it into the midst of the street thereof, and shalt burn with fire the city, and all the spoil thereof every whit, for the Lord thy God: and it shall be an heap for ever; it shall not be built again.

And there shall cleave nought of the cursed thing to thine hand: that the Lord may turn from the fierceness of his anger, and shew thee mercy, and have compassion upon thee, and multiply thee, as he hath sworn unto thy fathers;

Deuteronomy 13:12-17

This is the first mention of *Belial* in the Word of God. The Lord identifies the men that would attempt to lead His people away from Him to serve other gods as "children of Belial".

Children of Belial indicates the individuals that were under the control of Belial. They were being used by Belial to draw the people of God away from Him to serve other gods. It is interesting to note that the word *idol* is the Hebrew word *eliyl* which means "good for nothing, vain or vanity, of no value, thing of nought." This can be summed up in one word - WORTHLESS.

Belial, which means *worthlessness*, tries to lead men astray to follow something that is worthless. Idols are worthless; they have no value, and they cannot satisfy. There is a principle of Bible study which we call the law of *first reference*. It is a law of Bible study that says whenever a subject or a particular word is *first mentioned* in the Bible, there are some important principles that will be found concerning that subject or word.

The *first principle* we see in connection with Belial is that he attempts to draw people away from worshipping the true God. Under Belial are spirits that will SEDUCE people and draw them away from the Lord.

The Apostle Paul prophesied that *"in the latter times some shall depart from the faith, giving heed to SEDUCING spirits; and doctrines of devils"* (1 Timothy 4:1). The Taylor translation of this verse says, *"some in the church will turn away from Christ."* This is known as APOSTASY.

Webster defines *apostasy* as "abandonment of a previous loyalty, defection." I believe this is the reason why so many churches and some denominations have abandoned the faith. Some are considering ordaining homosexuals as ministers. What an abomination! This is no doubt the work of Belial and seducing spirits to cause many to *Apostatize*.

To *seduce* means to lead away, to persuade to disobedience or disloyalty, to lead astray by persuasion or false promises, to attract, to lure.

Chapter 2

BELIAL WORKS WITH JEZEBEL

Notwithstanding I have a few things against thee, because thou sufferest that woman Jezebel, which calleth herself a prophetess, to TEACH and to SEDUCE my servants to commit fornication, and to eat things sacrificed unto idols.

Revelation 2:20

Belial works with *the spirit of Jezebel* to seduce the servants of the Lord into fornication and idolatry. Jezebel can manifest through false teachings, and it is a seducing spirit.

Again, the intent is to draw people away from the truth and cause them to go into error, bringing upon themselves the judgment of God.

Behold, I will cast her into a bed, and them that commit adultery with her into great tribulation, except they repent of their deeds.

And I will kill her children with death; and all the churches shall know that I am he which searcheth the reins and hearts: and I will give unto every one of you according to your works.

Revelation 2:22,23

This was the judgment of the Lord upon those who allowed themselves to be seduced by the teachings of Jezebel.

Fornication and adultery will always be judged by the Lord.

Marriage is honourable in all, and the bed undefiled: but WHOREMONGERS AND ADULTERERS GOD WILL JUDGE.

Hebrews 13:4

Marriage is under attack in America like never before. Divorce is no longer considered unacceptable, but it is almost expected. Jezebel is a seducing spirit that draws people into *whoredom* and *adultery*. This will bring the judgment of God.

Whoredom means *prostitution*. It also means faithless, unworthy or idolatrous practices or pursuits (Webster). To *whore* means a faithless, unworthy or idolatrous desire, to *debauch*. Recently, a visiting minister was ministering in our church and began to prophetically identify spirits operating in our region. As he was prophesying, he mentioned in the prophecy the spirit of DEBAUCHERY. I took note as the word "debauchery" stayed with me months after the meeting.

I knew that the Lord, through this prophet, was identifying a spirit we had to bind in our region. To *debauch* means to seduce from chastity, to lead away from virtue or excellence, to corrupt by intemperance or sensuality (Webster).

There you have it. Spirits of whoredom, prostitution, and debauchery work under the strongman Belial. *Debauchery* is defined as extreme indulgence in sensuality." To be *sensual* means to be fleshly or carnal, deficient in moral, spiritual, or intellectual interests: irreligious.

It is interesting to note that the only reference to Belial in the New Testament is found in 2 Corinthians 6:15. Paul was dealing with the rampant carnality in the church of Corinth.

Jezebel does not work alone. Belial works with Jezebel to draw people into abominable sins including sodomy, homosexuality, incest, rape and perversion of all kinds (more on this later). Jezebel works through both *manipulation* and *intimidation*. If the spirit of Jezebel cannot manipulate people into sin, then intimidation will manifest. Jezebel threatened the prophet Elijah with death. Jezebel hates true apostles and prophets of God.

The greatest threat to Jezebel's influence has always been true servants of God. Those who preach the truth and maintain a standard of holiness are obstacles to the work of Jezebel. This spirit therefore attacks these men and women of God in order to move them out of the way.

Chapter 3
BELIAL SEARS THE CONSCIENCE

And she wrote in the letters, saying, Proclaim a fast, and set Naboth on high among the people:

And set two men, sons of Belial, before him, to bear witness against him, saying, Thou didst blaspheme God and the king....

And there came in two men, children of Belial, and sat before him: and the men of Belial witnessed against him, even against Naboth, in the presence of the people, saying, Naboth did blaspheme God and the king. Then they carried him forth out of the city, and stoned him with stones, that he died.

Then they sent to Jezebel, saying, Naboth is stoned, and is dead.

1 Kings 21:9,10,13,14

Here is an example of Jezebel and Belial working together. The men of Belial were evidently hired to bear false witness against Naboth. The Taylor translation says, "Then two men who had NO CONSCIENCE accused him." *Belial causes men to act without conscience.*

Paul further states there would be those who would be *"speaking lies in hypocrisy; having their conscience seared with a hot iron"* (1 Timothy 4:2).

The Phillips translation says, *"whose consciences are as dead as seared flesh."* The New English Bible says, *"branded with the devil's sign."* The Amplified Bible says *"whose consciences are seared (cauterized)."*

To *cauterize* means to deaden. One of the ways Belial is able to cause men to commit vile acts is by cauterizing the conscience. Men without a conscience are capable of committing any act without feeling remorse.

Every person is born with a conscience. The enemy must neutralize the conscience before seducing men to commit certain sins. According to Titus 1:15, *"the mind and conscience can be defiled."* To *defile* means to contaminate or make unclean. This is obviously a reference to evil spirits operating in the conscience.

When the conscience is seared, men and women are opened to all kinds of unclean spirits and capable of all kinds of unclean acts. There are many today who no longer feel that homosexuality, lesbianism, and incest are wrong.

Belial has cauterized the conscience to accept these things as acceptable lifestyles. When the conscience has been seared, men are capable of the vilest and most sickening acts. There is almost no limit to the depravity that men can exhibit when the conscience has been seared.

Chapter 4
BELIAL AND THE SPIRITS
OF RAPE AND SEXUAL ABUSE

Now as they were making their hearts merry, behold, the men of the city, certain SONS OF BELIAL, beset the house round about, and beat at the door, and spake to the master of the house, the old man, saying, Bring forth the man that came into thine house, that we may know him.

And the man, the master of the house, went out unto them, and said unto them, Nay, my brethren, nay, I pray you, do not so wickedly; seeing that this man is come into mine house, do not this folly.

Behold, here is my daughter a maiden, and his concubine; them I will bring out now, and humble ye them, and do with them what seemeth good unto you: but unto this man do not so VILE A THING.

But the men would not hearken to him: so the man took his concubine, and brought her forth unto them; and they knew her, and ABUSED her all the night until the morning....

Judges 19:22-25

The Berkeley translation says, *"They raped her and abused her."* This is one of the VILEST acts recorded in the Word of God. The "sons of Belial" raped the concubine until the next morning. As we continue reading through to the end of the chapter, we find that the concubine actually *died* from this vile act committed against her. She was literally RAPED TO DEATH.

Then came the woman in the dawning of the day, and fell down at the door of the man's house where her lord was, till it was light.

And her lord rose up in the morning, and opened the doors of the house, and went out to go his way: and, behold, the woman his concubine was fallen down at the door of the house, and her hands were upon the threshold.

And he said unto her, Up, and let us be going.   But none answered....

Judges 19:26-28

The Septuagint version says, *"She made no answer, for she was dead."*   The Knox version says, *"When no answer came, he knew that she was dead."*

And when he was come into his house, he took a knife, and laid hold on his concubine, and divided her, together with her bones, into twelve pieces, and sent her into all the coasts of Israel.

And it was so, that all that saw it said, There WAS NO SUCH DEED DONE NOR SEEN FROM THE DAY THE CHILDREN OF ISRAEL CAME UP OUT OF THE LAND OF EGYPT UNTO THIS DAY: consider of it, take advice, and speak your minds.

Judges 19:29,30

The Moffat translation says, *"was ever such a crime committed."*   The Jerusalem version says, *"has any man seen such a thing."*   The Berkeley translation says, *"Nothing like this has ever happened."*

This abominable act caused civil war in Israel.   The tribes of Israel gathered against the city of Gibeah to destroy it.

> *And I took my concubine, and cut her in pieces, and sent her throughout all the country of the inheritance of Israel: for they have committed LEWDNESS and FOLLY in Israel.*

Judges 20:6

The Word of God calls this act "lewdness". Webster defines *lewd* as "evil, wicked, sexually unchaste or licentious, obscene, salacious." And the word *obscene* means "disgusting to the senses, repulsive." Thus, Belial causes men to commit vile and obscene acts.

Other spirits working under Belial include rape and sexual abuse. The concubine was raped and abused until she died as a result. The proliferation of rape and sexual abuse, including *incest* and *sodomy*, are the result of the wicked spirit of Belial.

I have ministered to thousands of women and men who were the victims of sexual abuse as children. I also have cast out *spirits of death* that came in during the violation. When someone is violated in this way, it can be like a death coming into their souls. Sexual abuse is rampant in our nation. These filthy spirits are the work of the wicked ruler, Belial.

> *So all the men of Israel were gathered against the city, knit together as one man.*

> *And the tribes of Israel sent men through all the tribe of Benjamin, saying, What wickedness is this that is done among you?*

> *Now therefore deliver us the men, the CHILDREN OF BELIAL, which are in Gibeah, THAT WE MAY PUT THEM TO DEATH, and put away evil from Israel.*

Judges 20:11-13

13

The tribes of Israel were so repulsed by this act of mass rape that they gathered together against the city of Gibeah and demanded those who were guilty of this act. They decided to put to death the guilty.

There is much controversy today in America concerning the *death penalty*. Many liberals in our nation think it is a cruel method that needs to be outlawed. However, in the Word of God, there were sins that were abominable enough to merit the death penalty.

This book is not debating the pros and cons of the death penalty, but suffice it to say that it is found in the Word of God.

The *spirit of Belial* desires for us to tolerate these vile acts in our nation. But there are some sins that are so vile and abominable until it will stir moral indignation in most people, saved or unsaved.

As we continue the study of Belial, we are identifying spirits that operate under him. We can include spirits of *rape, incest, molestation, sexual abuse, sexual impurity, uncleanness, filthiness, lasciviousness, sodomy, lewdness, and obscenity.*

Chapter 5
BELIAL AND THE SPIRITS
OF ALCOHOL AND DRUNKENNESS

Now Hannah, she spake in her heart; only her lips moved, but her voice was not heard: therefore ELI THOUGHT SHE HAD BEEN DRUNKEN.

And Eli said unto her, How long wilt thou BE DRUNKEN? put away thy wine from thee.

And Hannah answered and said, No, my lord, I am a woman of a sorrowful spirit: I have drunk neither wine nor strong drink, but have poured out my soul before the Lord.

Count not thine handmaid for a daughter of BELIAL: for out of the abundance of my complaint and grief have I spoken hitherto.

1 Samuel 1:13-16

The spirit of Belial operates through *alcohol and drunkenness*. Drunkenness is a way to break down the morals and open people up to *lust and perversion*. I believe that spirits of alcohol and drunkenness operate under the strongman of Belial.

It is a known fact that many children of alcoholic parents are often the victims of sexual abuse, including incest. Alcohol can also open the door for *spirits of rape* including "date rape" (that is so prevalent on many of the college campuses).

Look not thou upon the wine when it is red, when it giveth his colour in the cup, when it moveth itself aright.

At the last it biteth like a serpent, and stingeth like an adder.

Thine eyes shall behold strange women, and thine heart shall utter perverse things.

Proverbs 23:31-33

These verses show the connection of the spirit of perversion to drunkenness. To *pervert* means to cause to turn aside or away from what is good or true or morally right, to corrupt, to cause to turn aside from what is generally done or accepted.

Sexual perversion has become rampant in our nation with the promotion of homosexuality and lesbianism as acceptable and alternate lifestyles. These are *perversions* according to the Word of God. Spirits of perversion, including homosexuality and lesbianism, operate under the strongman of Belial. This is also referred to in the Word of God as *sodomy*.

Sodomy is defined as copulation with a member of the same sex or with an animal (bestiality). It is also non-coital, especially anal or oral copulation with a member of the opposite sex (Webster). The term "sodomite" is mentioned five times in the Old Testament.

Sodomites were temple prostitutes that were a part of the worship of the idol gods of fertility in Canaan. These vile acts were a part of the idol worship of the Canaanites.

THE SONS OF ELI

Now the sons of Eli were sons of Belial; they knew not the Lord.

1 Samuel 2:12

Now Eli was very old, and heard all that his sons did unto all Israel; and how they lay with the women that assembled at the door of the tabernacle of the congregation.

1 Samuel 2:22

The sons of Eli represent *ministry*. They, along with Eli, were in charge of the priesthood, regulating the temple, and the sacrifices of Israel.

Their abuses brought the judgment of the Lord upon them, and the establishment of a new order under Samuel. These sons are called *"sons of Belial"*. They were being motivated and controlled by the spirit of Belial.

One of the works of Belial is to bring uncleanness into the temple of God. The ministry is a target of this spirit. He desires to draw the servant of the Lord, His anointed, into sin (especially sexual sin) to bring reproach to the church.

These priests were also guilty of greed in making themselves "fat with the chiefest of all the offerings of Israel" (1 Samuel 2:29). Their sin was so great that "men abhorred the offering of the Lord" (1 Samuel 2:17).

...Notwithstanding they hearkened not unto the voice of their father, because the Lord would SLAY THEM.
1 Samuel 2:25

The Rotherham translation says, *"...for Yahweh was pleased to put them to death."* The Lord judged their sin with death. There is no reason for this kind of activity, especially from those who are in the ministry. God forbid that men of God would lay with the women of their congregations.

The spirit of Belial desires to draw the servants of God into this kind of hideous activity in order to bring judgment upon the servants of the Lord. The sons of Eli knew not the Lord. True apostles, prophets, evangelists, pastors and teachers know the Lord. They also know that there are moral standards to which God's servants are expected to live.

Remember, whoremongers and adulterers God will judge.

For I have told him that I will judge his house for ever for the iniquity which he knoweth; because his sons made themselves vile, and he restrained them not.

1 Samuel 3:13

This verse tells us the Lord considered their acts VILE. The Berkeley translation says, *"that his sons were bringing a curse upon themselves."* The Revised Standard version says, *"because his sons were blaspheming God."*

Again, the work of Belial is to cause men to get involved in sins that are abominable and bring the curse of God.

Who knowing the judgment of God, that they which commit such things are WORTHY OF DEATH, not only do the same, but have pleasure in them that do them.

Romans 1:32

What sins do Paul mention that are worthy of death? The answer is *idolatry, homosexuality and lesbianism.* Now I am not stating that every person involved in these sins should be put to death. Thank God for His mercy. There is salvation offered to all. Jesus died and shed His blood for sin. Those who repent and accept His sacrifices will receive deliverance and forgiveness of sin.

However, the judgment of God does come to those who, through a hard and impenitent heart, will not repent (Romans 2:5).

Regardless of what the secular media tries to tell us concerning homosexuality and lesbianism, these are perversions and are under the judgment of God.

For this cause God gave them up unto vile affections: for even their women did change the natural use into that which is against nature:

And likewise also the men, leaving the natural use of the woman, burned in their lust one toward another; men with men working that which is unseemly, and receiving in themselves that recompence of their error which was meet.

Romans 1:26-27

The Phillips translation says, *"disgraceful passions".* The Knox version says, *"passions which brought dishonor to themselves."* The Conybeare translation says, *"men with men working abomination."*

Webster's definition of *abomination* is "extreme disgust and hatred, loathing." To *loathe* means to dislike greatly and often with disgust or intolerance, to detest.

19

And even as they did not like to retain God in their knowledge, God gave them over to a reprobate mind, to do those things which are not convenient;

Romans 1:28

Reprobate spirits also operate with homosexuality and perversion. The dictionary definition of *reprobate* is "rejected as worthless, morally abandoned, depraved." You will recall that the definition of Belial is WORTHLESSNESS.

When something is reprobate it has been judged by God as worthless and, therefore, rejected. The Revised Standard version says, *"God gave them up to a base mind;"* and the word *base* means to be of little value. Synonyms include *low* and *vile* meaning "deserving contempt because of the absence of higher values, disgusting depravity or filth."

Belial is a wicked ruler that leads men into sins that are base and vile. Reprobate spirits and spirits of homosexuality and lesbianism operate under Belial causing men to commit vile acts, thus bringing the judgment of God.

The Apostle Paul goes on to mention a host of evil spirits that come in once the mind becomes reprobate.

Being filled with all unrighteousness, fornication, wickedness, covetousness, maliciousness; full of envy, murder, debate, deceit, malignity; whisperers,

Backbiters, haters of God, despiteful, proud, boasters, inventors of evil things, disobedient to parents,

> *Without understanding, covenantbreakers, without natural affection, implacable, unmerciful:*
>
> *Romans 1:29-31*

This verse says that they are FILLED with these things. This is obviously a list of demons that enter and dwell in those who are guilty of *base sins*. In other words, those guilty of these sins had become demonized.

Unclean sexual acts attract unclean spirits. The only solution is repentance and deliverance.

Chapter 6

BELIAL: REJECTING THE LORD'S ANOINTED

And Saul also went home to Gibeah; and there went with him a band of men, whose hearts God had touched.

But the children of Belial said, How shall this man save us? And they despised him, and brought him no presents. But he held his peace.

1 Samuel 10:26-27

And there happened to be there a man of Belial whose name was Sheba, the son of Bichri, a Benjamite: and he blew a trumpet, and said, We have no part in David, neither have we inheritance in the son of Jesse...

2 Samuel 20:1

Another manifestation of Belial is to reject the Lord's anointed. This is a *spirit of irreverence* and disrespect for the ones that are sent by God. Belial hates the anointed of the Lord. God's anointed bring deliverance to the people. The Young's Literal translation of 2 Samuel 20:1 calls Sheba "a man of worthlessness." The Amplified version calls him "base and contemptible fellow."

Those controlled by Belial will despise the Lord's anointed. To *despise* means to look down on with contempt or aversion, to regard as negligible, worthless, or distasteful. This was the attitude of those controlled by Belial toward David, the Lord's anointed.

The Basic English translation of 1 Samuel 10:27 says, *"And having no respect for him, they gave him no offering."* Belial will cause individuals to not support men and women sent by the Lord. They will withhold their financial support.

It is important to honor and respect those who are called and sent by the Lord. One of the ways we honor them is to support them financially and to bless them with our words. It is dangerous to touch the Lord's anointed. As we receive the Lord's anointed, we will receive the fullness and blessing of the Lord.

Belial hates the Lord's anointed. Preachers and teachers anointed by God are a hindrance to Belial's work. Godly leaders call men to repentance and a lifestyle of righteousness.

They bring deliverance and restoration to the people of God. They are a restraining influence to the work of Belial.

NABAL

Now therefore know and consider what thou wilt do; for evil is determined against our master, and against all his household: for he is such a son of BELIAL, THAT A MAN CANNOT SPEAK TO HIM.

1 Samuel 25:17

Let not my lord, I pray thee, regard this man of Belial, even Nabal: for as his name is, so is he; Nabal is his name, and folly is with him: ...

1 Samuel 25:25

The name *Nabal* means base, churl, fool, or brute. Nabal, the husband of Abigail, endangered his whole family by speaking harshly to David. David was so angered by Nabal's response to his request for assistance that he determined to kill Nabal and his family.

David had protected Nabal's possessions and had respected his shepherds who watched his sheep. Nabal, in return, disrespected David by answering him harshly.

And Nabal answered David's servants, and said, Who is David? and who is the son of Jesse? there be many servants now a days that break away every man from his master.

1 Samuel 25:10

This is another example of how the spirit of Belial causes men to disrespect the Lord's anointed. Nabal said, "Who is David?"

Everyone in Israel knew who David was. He was the champion of Israel. He had delivered them from the hands of the Philistines by defeating Goliath.

However, Nabal accused David of being a rebellious servant. 1 Samuel 25:14 says, "... he railed on them." This is speaking of Nabal's treatment of the servants of David. He treated them with contempt. He insulted them. He scoffed at them. He flared out at them.

Nabal was a wealthy man, yet he refused to give to the Lord's anointed. The Word of God says he was "very great"

(1 Samuel 25:2). He possessed "three thousand sheep and a thousand goats".

The name Nabal means "churl". Webster's definition of *churl* means "a rude, ill-bred person, or stingy morose person." To be *churlish* means to be vulgar, ill-natured, difficult to work with or deal with.

Abigail referred to her husband as a "man of Belial". She knew that her husband was unapproachable and that no one could speak to him. The Rotherham translation says, *"he is such an abandoned man, that one cannot speak to him."*

The Basic English version says, *"he is such a good-for-nothing person."* The Know version says, *"he is so cross-grained a man that there is no reasoning with him."* The word "cross-grained" means difficult to deal with.

As much as we like to see good in everyone, there are unfortunately people in the world like Nabal. Can you imagine what Abigail had to deal with being married to this man? It was only because of her wisdom that her life and the lives of her loved ones were saved. She is an example of the power of *intercession.*

And it came to pass about ten days after, that the Lord smote Nabal, and he died.

1 Samuel 25:38

The American Translation says, *"the Lord inflicted a stroke upon."* This was after Nabal held a feast in his home, like the feast of a king. He was a stingy, selfish, and irreverent man. He did not respect the anointing upon King David. The Lord's judgment came upon him, and he died. David stated: *"...for the Lord hath returned the wickedness of Nabal upon his own head"* (1 Samuel 25:39).

Chapter 7
BELIAL: CURSING GOD'S ANOINTED

And when king David came to Bahurim, behold, thence came out a man of the family of the house of Saul, whose name was Shimei, the son of Gera: he came forth, and cursed still as he came.

And he cast stones at David, and at all the servants of king David: and all the people and all the mighty men were on his right hand and on his left.

And thus said Shimei when he cursed, Come out, come out, thou bloody man, and thou man of Belial:

2 Samuel 16:5-7

Shimei was calling king David a worthless man. The Basic English version says, *"You good for nothing."* David was fleeing from his rebellious son, Absalom, when he encountered Shimei.

Shimei was from the family of the house of Saul and was no doubt angry at the fact that David had succeeded Saul as king. This is just like the enemy to accuse God's anointed. The Pharisees said Jesus cast out devils by Beelzebub.

They were accusing him of using Satan's power to deliver people. To call someone a "man of Belial" is to call them worthless, no good, wicked, base and vile. Shimei was accusing David of being a rebellious murderer who was responsible for Saul's fall. This is another example of how this spirit will attack and accuse the Lord's anointed.

But Abishai the son of Zeruiah answered and said, Shall not Shimei be put to death for this, BECAUSE HE CURSED THE LORD'S ANOINTED?

2 *Samuel 19:21*

After David was returned to his position in Jerusalem, Shimei came to him and repented of what he said. Abishai desired to have him put to death for cursing the Lord's anointed. David, however, had mercy upon Shimei and did not put him to death.

David understood the judgment that would come upon those who touched the Lord's anointed. He refused to touch Saul even though his life was in danger. In the case of Shimei, mercy prevailed even judgment because of Shimei's *repentant* attitude.

Strong intercessors help cover the men and women of God from the attacks of Belial. A *curse* is an evil word spoken against a person or a thing. Words spoken against the servants of God are spiritual arrows sent by the enemy to hurt and destroy. They are what the Word refers to as the *"fiery darts of the wicked"* (Ephesians 6:16).

David understood the spiritual warfare the Lord's anointed must face when men curse. David prays in Psalm 64:2-3, *"Hide me from the secret counsel of the wicked; from the insurrection of the workers of iniquity. Who whet their tongue like a sword, and bend their bows to shoot their arrows, even bitter words:"*

These words are *witchcraft attacks* against the servants of the Lord. They are spiritual missiles directed towards the

Lord's anointed. Life and death are in the power of the tongue (Proverbs 18:21). This is one of the methods Belial uses to direct his assault against the servants of the Lord.

Chapter 8
BELIAL: UNTHOUGHTFUL AND INCONSIDERATE

Then answered all the WICKED MEN AND MEN OF BELIAL, of those that went with David, and said, Because they went not with us, we will not give them ought of the spoil that we have recovered, save to every man his wife and his children, that they may lead them away, and depart.

1 Samuel 30:22

After David pursued the Amalekites from Ziklag and recovered the spoil, certain men of Belial manifested a selfish attitude toward the ones who could not continue in the battle because of weariness. David's attitude was to part the spoil equally among all the army.

David considered all of those in his band. The men of Belial were selfish and only concerned about themselves. Belial causes men to be selfish and unconcerned about others. This was the same attitude manifested by Nabal. He was greedy and selfish and manifested an attitude that was worthless.

The Knox translation calls them *"churlish, graceless fellows."* Webster defines *graceless* as "immoral, unregenerate, devoid of attractive qualities." On the other hand, to be *gracious* means to be considerate or thoughtful.

Those influenced and controlled by Belial are inconsiderate and unthoughtful about the needs and condition of others. The apostle Paul mentioned men who were **without natural affection, implacble, and unmerciful.**

The Weymouth translation says, *"without affection, and without pity."* Moffat says, *"calloused, merciless."* Goodspeed says, *"unloving and unpitying."* The Revised Standard says, *"heartless and ruthless."*

COLD LOVE

And because iniquity shall abound, the love of many shall wax cold.

Matthew 24:12

This is a condition known as *cold love*. This is the result of iniquity. The word "iniquity" in this verse means *lawlessness*. Iniquity causes men to lose their compassion and tenderness. It causes men to become calloused and merciless. Other spirits that work with "cold love" are *betrayal* and *treachery*. These are end-time spirits.

Belial is an *end-time* spirit that will cause iniquity and lawlessness to abound. "End-time" does not mean this spirit has not been in existence before. It simply means it will be in strong manifestation in the last days.

Other terms to describe *cold love* are: to be pitiless, ruthless, have no compassion, have no pity, show no mercy, harden one's heart.

Chapter 9
THE FLOODS OF BELIAL

When the waves of death compassed me, the floods of ungodly men made me afraid.

2 Samuel 22:5

The literal translation of this verse is "the floods of Belial". This verse is a portion of a song David sang in the day the Lord delivered him out of the hand of all his enemies, and out of the hand of Saul.

The American Standard version says, *"the floods of ungodliness made me afraid."* Belial has released a flood of ungodliness upon our nation.

Ungodly is defined as denying God or disobedient to Him: impious, irreligious, contrary to moral law, sinful, wicked.

Belial is responsible for the flood of ungodliness manifested through Hollywood, television, and the mass media. Belial is responsible for rebellion and disobedience to God. This spirit has caused many to be irreligious and impious.

No reverence - no fear of God - is the result of Belial's influence. To *flood* means to cover, to inundate, to fill abundantly or excessively. Belial desires to cover the earth with filth and immorality. This flood also includes the persecution that comes against the Lord's anointed, David.

Belial desires to murder and destroy the Lord's anointed. He is a strongman that attacks ministers and churches. The American translation says, *"the torrents of perdition assailed me."* We find that the word *torrent* is defined as "an outpouring, a rush."

Perdition means destruction. Spirits of *death and destruction* work with Belial to assail the servants of God. We have already seen that Jezebel works under Belial to destroy true servants of God. Lies, slander, seduction, lust, and pride are all weapons used against the Lord's anointed.

It is important to intercede against Belial's work. When the enemy shall come in like a flood, the Spirit of the Lord will lift up a standard against him. The Lord will lift up a standard against the floods of Belial. The prayers and intercessions of God's people will be a standard against this flood.

Chapter 10
COMING AGAINST BELIAL

But the SONS OF BELIAL shall be all of them as thorns thrust away, because they cannot be taken with hands:

But the man that shall touch them must be fenced with iron and the staff of a spear; and they shall be utterly burned with fire in the same place.

2 Samuel 23:6,7

This verse compares the "sons of Belial" to thorns that cannot be handled. Those who deal with Belial "must be fenced with iron and the staff of a spear." A *thorn* is something that causes distress or irritation. To be *thorny* means to be full of difficulties or controversial points.

This verse pronounces the judgment upon Belial and those who follow him: *"they shall be utterly burned with fire in the same place."* This is a reference to eternal damnation in hell-fire. I believe that Belial is a spirit that will cause many to die lost and spend eternity in hell.

"Fenced with iron and the staff of a spear" is a reference to putting on the whole armor of God. We cannot deal with this spirit without the whole armor of God.

The Lord is raising up intercessors and preachers to come against this spirit in the last days. This is an *end-time spirit* assigned to corrupt the earth, but the Lord has an *end-time people* to combat him. The Young Literal translation says, *"And the man who cometh against them."*

David had to fight and overcome the men controlled by Belial. David is a type of the New Testament church. He is a type of the prophetic church the Lord is raising up in this hour. Just as David overcame, we will also overcome this end-time spirit.

We will not handle this spirit with our natural hands, he is too thorny and difficult for that. But we must and will attack him in the power of the Spirit, wearing the whole armor of God.

Chapter 11
BELIAL AND SPIRITS OF INFIRMITY

An evil disease, say they, cleaveth fast unto him: and now that he lieth he shall rise up no more.

Psalm 41:8

This verse literally reads, *"a thing of Belial cleaveth unto him."* Fatal diseases were considered a thing of Belial. The Revised Standard version says, *"A deadly thing has fastened upon him; he will not rise again where he lies."*

Belial also has a host of spirits of infirmity and sickness that operate under him. Wherever there is immorality, there will be sickness and disease. These are curses that come upon those who are perverse and crooked. Remember, Belial desires to draw men into sin, immorality and perversion in order to bring the curse of the Lord upon a nation.

Whoremongers and adulterers, God will judge (Hebrews 13:4). It is possible that AIDS is a thing of Belial that cleaves unto a person. AIDS is undoubtedly the result of sin, homosexuality, fornication, perversion, and drug abuse. AIDS is fatal and in the natural, there is no cure. The Taylor translation says, *"It's fatal, whatever it is."* They say, "He'll never get out of that bed!"

The context of Psalm 41 is again the attacks of Belial against David, the Lord's anointed. David states, *"All that hate me whisper together against me: against me do they devise my hurt"* (Psalm 41:7). Again Belial is mentioned in this context.

I believe that as an end-time spirit, Belial has been released by the enemy to attack ministry gifts.

These can also include attacks of *witchcraft* against true servants of the Lord, which often manifest through sickness. Leaders need strong prayer support against these spirits that are released under the strongman, Belial, who hates and seeks to destroy ministry gifts.

Chapter 12
BELIAL AND PORNOGRAPHY

I will set no wicked thing before mine eyes: I hate the work of them that turn aside, it shall not cleave to me.

Psalm 101:3

The Harrison translation says, *"I will not have anything unworthy in my presence..."*

This shows us the attitude and abhorrence we as people of God should have toward anything related to Belial. Anything base, vile, unworthy, unclean, ungodly, contemptible, wicked, blasphemous or shameful, we should resist and abhor.

We are to abhor that which is evil, and cleave to that which is good. *Abhor* is a strong word. It means to regard with extreme repugnance, to loathe; to turn aside or keep away from especially in scorn or shuddering fear, to reject, to hate.

This verse can apply to the present day rise of pornography and the sexual filth that Belial is flooding our nation with. One of the vilest forms of pornography is "kiddie porn" which is a thriving business supported by pedophiles. *Pedophilia* is sexual perversion in which children are the preferred sexual object.

Most states have obscenity laws that are being challenged by those who feel as if government should provide no constraint. *Obscenity* is defined as the state of being obscene. *Obscene* means disgusting to the senses, repulsive, abhorrent to morality or virtue (Webster).

Pornography opens the door for a host of evil spirits of lust and perversion. There has also been a connection between pornography and rape in some studies. I believe Belial is a ruling spirit over spirits of pornography, whoredom, prostitution and other sexual spirits.

Sexual impurity is another strong spirit that is under his control including spirits of homosexuality and lesbianism (perversion). If this spirit can pervert the morals of a nation through sexual immorality, he can bring the judgment and curse of the Lord upon a nation.

Chapter 13
BELIAL AND WICKED PLOTS

An ungodly man diggeth up evil: and in his lips there is as a burning fire.

Proverbs 16:27

The American Standard Version says, *"A worthless man deviseth mischief,..."* The Berkeley version says, *"A worthless man plots harm,..."* To *devise* means to plan to bring about. A *plot* is a secret plan for accomplishing a usually evil or unlawful end.

Belial causes men to plan and plot that which is evil. Psalm 37:12 says, *"the wicked plotteth against the just."* There are people involved in forms of witchcraft that are planning to destroy the Church. We have heard reports of witches fasting to break up marriages of Christian leaders and to disrupt the Church.

It is almost hard to believe that there are actually people this wicked. I believe it because the Word of God states it. Most people would be shocked to know the types of gross sins and plots taking place behind closed doors.

Psalm 37:32 says, *"The wicked watcheth the righteous, and seeketh to slay him."* The Berkeley translation says, *"The wicked lies in wait for the righteous, and seeks to put him to death."* The New American Bible says, *The wicked man spies on the just and seeks to slay him."*

What a sobering thought! No wonder the Word of God admonishes us to be *sober and vigilant*. Belial will influence men to plot against the righteous.

Chapter 14
THE MIND OF BELIAL:
LAWLESSNESS AND REBELLION

There is one come out of thee, that imagineth evil against the Lord, a wicked counsellor.

Nahum 1:11

The Jerusalem translation says, *"From you has sprung one who plots evil against Yahweh, a man with the MIND OF BELIAL."*

Nahum is prophesying judgment against Nineveh and the Assyrian Empire. The king of Assyria was actually plotting against the Lord. The Taylor translation says, *"Who is this king of yours who dares plot against the Lord?"*

This is the spirit of *Antichrist*. Psalm 2:2-3 says, *"The kings of the earth set themselves, and the rulers take counsel together, against the Lord, and against his anointed, saying, Let us break their bands asunder, and cast away their cords from us."*

There you have it, the ultimate goal of Belial - TO CAST OFF RESTRAINT. The Church is a restraining force in the earth against the filth and ungodliness Belial desires to flood upon the earth.

The Amplified Bible says, *"and cast their cords (of control) from us."* These are the spirits of *lawlessness and rebellion.* Where there is no law, people run wild. Our entire judicial system was founded on the Judeo-Christian ethic found in the Bible.

In other words, the Bible is the foundation of our legal system. A society that rejects the Bible as its moral authority will eventually have problems with its judicial system. Belial hates the restraining power of the Bible, the Holy Spirit, and the Church. This is why he attacks them so viciously.

Belial desires immorality and ungodliness to reign without any restraint. Belial is responsible for an attack upon our judicial system. Laws against homosexuality, lesbianism and adultery, which were once a part of our legal code, are now removed.

Homosexuals believe they have a right to live ungodly lifestyles. Many are clamoring, "Leave me alone, and let me do what I want. I don't want any preacher to tell me what is right and wrong;" and, "Separation of church and state, take prayer out of the schools." This is all an attempt to cast off restraint.

Chapter 15
BELIAL AND UNGODLY SOUL TIES

Be ye not unequally yoked together with unbelievers: for what fellowship hath righteousness with unrighteousness? and what communion hath light with darkness?

And what concord hath Christ with Belial? or what part hath he that believeth with an infidel?

2 Corinthians 6:14,15

When there is an unequal yoke between believers and unbelievers, we call this an *ungodly soul tie*. Breaking ungodly soul ties is a key to deliverance. Ungodly association causes evil spirits to be transferred. If Belial cannot directly control you, he will influence you through ungodly association.

Associating with the wrong people can cause you to receive an *evil transfer* of spirits. One of the keys to being delivered from Belial's control is to break every ungodly soul tie and obey the Word of God which says, *"be not unequally yoked together with unbelievers."*

The Williams translation says, *"STOP forming intimate and inconsistent relations with unbelievers."* This is the only time the name "Belial" is mentioned in the New Testament. I believe the Spirit of God chose this word to bring revelation to a spirit that the church **must not, in any way,** be in fellowship with.

Verse 15 ties Belial with unrighteousness, darkness, infidels, and idoiatry. The first reference to Belial in the Word of God ties him to *idolatry*. The Corinthians had been saved from a lifestyle of idolatry.

As stated before, I believe that Belial is an end-time spirit that will be an enemy of the Church. We are to separate ourselves from all uncleanness and filthiness that is associated with this ruling spirit.

The church at Corinth also had a problem with carnality. There was strife, envy, contention, sexual impurity, and even drunkenness taking place within the church. The apostle Paul wrote the letter to Corinth to correct these problems and to set things in order.

TOUCH NOT THE UNCLEAN THING

Wherefore come out from among them, and be ye separate, saith the Lord, and touch not the unclean thing; and I will receive you,

2 Corinthians 6:17

The Corinthians had come out of a lifestyle of idolatry. Paul admonishes them to separate themselves completely from their former lifestyle and to TOUCH NOT THE UNCLEAN THING.

The Knox version says, *"and do not even touch what is unclean."* As believers, we are not to TOUCH what is unclean. There are unclean spirits attached to what is unclean. The word *unclean* is defined as that which is *dirty and filthy*.

Idolatry is unclean. It is considered spiritual whoredom and adultery. It is departing from the Lord and breaking covenant. As the Lord's people, we are to keep ourselves away from all that is unclean.

Belial is associated with uncleanness. According to Galatians 5:19, uncleanness is a work of the flesh. We are not to allow uncleanness to be named once among us as saints (Ephesians 5:3). God has not called us unto uncleanness but unto HOLINESS (1 Thessalonians 4:7). These verses tie uncleanness to *fornication.*

Fornication is from the Greek word *porneia* meaning harlotry, adultery, incest, and idolatry. There was a man in Corinth that was guilty of sexual relations with his father's wife (1 Corinthians 5:11).

The Taylor translation says, *"something so wicked that even the heathen don't do it."* The Phillips version says, *"immorality of a kind that even pagans condemn."* This man was judged and turned over to Satan for the destruction of the flesh.

Again, the only time Belial is mentioned in the New Testament is in Paul's second letter to Corinth. Belial was obviously strong in the city of Corinth, and he was operating within the Church!

According to 2 Corinthians 7:1, we are to cleanse ourselves from all filthiness of the flesh and spirits, perfecting holiness in the fear of God. We must *loose ourselves* from Belial's influence if we are to live lives pleasing to God. **We must bind the strongman Belial and spoil his goods!**

Following is a list of spirits operating under Belial that we can attack and cast out.

Spirits Under the Strongman of Belial

Uncleanness	Treachery	Filthiness
Cold love	Fornication	Betrayal
Adultery	Blasphemy	Incest
Infirmity	Perversion	Sickness
Rape	Death	Destruction
Molestation	Lawlessness	Lesbianism
Rebellion	Abuse	Free love
Jezebel	Harlotry	Sorcery
Whoredom	Implacable	Prostitution
Unmerciful	Pornography	Iniquity
Irreverence	Obscenity	Idolatry
Alcohol	Shameless	Drunkenness
Immodest	Lust	Lying
Immorality	Deception	Debauchery
Apostasy	Witchcraft	Homosexuality
Sodomy	Heresy	Delusion
		Backsliding
		Drug addiction
		Hardness of heart
		Sexual impurity
		Seared conscience
		Doctrines of devils
		False teaching

Scripture References For Belial

Deuteronomy	**13:13(14)**	the children of *Belial*, (marg. naughty men)
	15:9	a thought of thy *wicked* heart
Judges	**19:22**	certain sons of *Belial*
	20:13	the children of *Belial*
1 Samuel	**1:16**	for a daughter of *Belial*
	2:12	the sons of Eli (were) sons of *Belial*
	10:27	But the children of *Belial* said
	25:17	for he (is such) a son of *Belial*
	25:25	regard this man of *Belial*
	30:22	and (men) of *Belial*
2 Samuel	**16:7**	thou man of *Belial*
	20:1	be there a man of *Belial*
	22:5	the floods of *ungodly men* (marg. Belial)
	23:6	But (the sons) of *Belial*
1 Kings	**21:10**	set two men, sons of *Belial*
	21:13	two men, children of *Belial* the men of *Belial* witnessed

Scripture References For Belial (cont'd)

2 Chronicles	**13:7**	vain men, the children of *Belial*
Job	**34:18**	say to a king, (Thou art) *wicked*?
Psalms	**18:4(5)**	the floods of *ungodly men* (marg. Belial)
	41:8(9)	An *evil* disease, (say they), cleaveth fast (marg. A thing of Belial)
	101:3	I will set no *wicked* thing before (marg. thing of Belial)
Proverbs	**6:12**	A *naughty* person
	16:27	An *ungodly* man diggeth up evil (marg. A witness of Belial)
	19:28	An *ungodly* witness scorneth (marg. A witness of Belial)
Nahum	**1:11**	a *wicked* counsellor (marg. counsellor of Belial)
	1:15 (2:1)	the *wicked* shall no more pass
2 Corinthians	**6:15**	what concord hath Christ with *Belial*

APPENDIX

Tactics to Rout Demons
(From <u>Annihilating the Hosts of Hell</u>, by Win Worley)

A Way for the Deliverance Worker to Get Started:

1. Brief conversations about the reason the person is there for ministry

2. General prayer and worship - focus on God and His goodness, power, etc.

3. Bind powers over the area, break assignments from powers in the air to demons in the person. Ask for angelic protection (Hebrews 1:14)

4. Ask and receive by faith the gifts of the Spirit needed to minister.

Leadership During Deliverance Time

1. Too many people commanding spirits (different ones) at the same time causes confusion for everyone, especially to the person being ministered to.

2. Leadership will often shift as the Holy Spirit directs.

3. Husbands are often the most effective in commanding spirits to leave their wives, with the support of others.

Tactics of Speaking to Demons

1. Address the spirit by name and if that is not known, address by *function*.
>   a. Either the Holy Spirit will give it, or
>   b. The demon will reveal himself.
>   c. Do not rely on either method exclusively- be open to the Holy Spirit in this area.

2. Repeatedly remind these spirits that your authority is given to you by Jesus Christ, Who is far above all rule and authority (Ephesians 1:21).

3. Remind them of their fate in Revelation 20:10 and other places in Scripture (Job 30:3-8). Use the statement ("The Lord Jesus Christ rebukes you") repeatedly as a battering ram.

4. It is helpful to harass the demons to confess that Jesus Christ is their Lord.

5. Ruler demons often can be badgered for more information.

6. At times you will command the ruler demon to go and then clean out the lesser demons under him, and if that does not work, reverse the tactics.

7. Bind and separate interfering spirits as God leads.

8. There is no need to shout at demons since the battle is not in the flesh but in the Spirit.

What to Expect in Receiving Deliverance

While many deliverances involve obvious physical manifestations, not all react in this manner. Some spirits leave quietly and non-violently.

You may not have a strong physical reaction when receiving deliverance, therefore, don't be disappointed if you don't receive in this manner. What you *should* expect is a release. You know there is a *release* when....

1. Oppressive force disappears;
2. Heaviness lifts;
3. Uneasiness goes away;
4. Burden or load lightens;
5. There is an inner sense of liberty, freedom, and divine satisfaction or contentment;
6. The joy of the Lord comes and you are able to rejoice;

The *result* of deliverance is righteousness, peace, and joy in the Holy Ghost (Romans 14:17). When devils are cast out, the Kingdom of God has come (Matthew 12:28).

Demon Manifestations

When evil spirits depart you can normally expect some sort of manifestation through the mouth or nose. Listed below are some of the common manifestations:

1. Coughing
2. Drooling
3. Vomiting
4. Spitting
5. Foaming
6. Crying
7. Screaming
8. Sighing
9. Roaring
10. Belching
11. Yawning
12. Exhaling

Again, when demons are cast out they normally leave through the mouth or the nose. Spirits are associated with breathing. Both the Hebrews and the Greeks had only one word for spirit and breath. In the Greek, that word is *pneuma*. The Holy Spirit is breathed in (John 20:22). Evil spirits are breathed out.

Sometimes people shake or tremble when they receive deliverance. Their body, in whole or part, may actually shake or tremble.

Hindrances to Receiving Deliverance

1. Curses
2. Sin
3. Pride
4. Passivity
5. Ungodly Soul Ties
6. Occultism
7. Fear
8. Embarrassment
9. Unbelief
10. Lack of Desire
11. Unforgiveness
12. Lack of Knowledge

All demons have legal, biblical grounds. They may *not* torment at will. If demons have legal grounds then they have the right to remain. These legal grounds must be destroyed in order to receive and maintain deliverance.

How to Keep Your Deliverance

1. Read God's Word daily.

2. Find a group of Bible believing people, preferably a church, and regularly meet with them for worship, study and ministry.

3. Pray with the understanding and in tongues.

4. Place the blood of Jesus on yourself and your family.

5. Determine as nearly as you can which spirits have been cast out of you. Make a list for these areas Satan will try to recapture.

6. The way demons gain re-entry is through a lax, undisciplined thought life. The mind is the battlefield. You must cast down imaginations, and bring every thought into the obedience of Christ (2 Corinthians 10:5).

7. Pray to the Father fervently, asking Him to make you alert, sober and vigilant against wrong thoughts (1 Peter 5:8, 9).

8. The demons signal their approach to you by the fact that the old thought patterns you once had are now trying to return unto you. As soon as this happens, immediately rebuke them. State *verbally* that you refuse them as quickly as possible.

9. You have the *authority* to loose the Angels of the Lord to battle the demons (Hebrews 1:14; Matthew 18:18). Bind the demons and loose upon them the spirits of destruction (1 Chronicles 21:12), burning and judgment (Isaiah 4:4), from the Lord Jesus Christ. Loose *warrior angels* upon the demons.

Crusaders Ministries
Book Catalog

Whoso loveth instruction loveth knowledge....
Proverbs 12:1

Written by John Eckhardt

List Price - $1.00

JEM12   **Deliverance The Children's Bread**

List Price - $3.00

JEM03   **The Ministry Anointing of Helps**

JEM05   **How to Put a Demand on the Anointing**

JEM06   **Releasing God's Power Through Laying On of Hands**

JEM09   **Momentum - The Key to Victory**

JEM14   **Let Us Alone**

List Price - $5.00

JEM01   **The Prophetic Flow**

JEM04   **The Ministry Anointing of the Prophet**

Crusaders Ministries

Book Catalog

Whoso loveth instruction loveth knowledge....
Proverbs 12:1

(Cont'd)

List Price - $5.00

JEM08	**The Ministry Anointing of the Apostle**
JEM10	**Identifying & Breaking Curses**
JEM11	**Behemoth & Leviathan**
JEM13	**50 Truths Concerning Apostolic Ministry**
JEM15	**Demon Hit List**

List Price - $10.00

JEM07 Warfare	**Deliverance & Spiritual Manual**

If you would like to schedule a speaking engagement or order
books and tapes by John Eckhardt
please write or call:

Crusaders Ministries
P.O. Box 7211
Chicago, Illinois 60680
(312) 637-2121

If you would like to order any of the books listed in our catalog please fill out the order form below. If you need more room please attach a separate sheet of paper.

Name: _____

Address: _____

_____

Phone: _____ day _____evening

Item no.	Quanity	Price ea.	Total
_____	_____	_____	_____
_____	_____	_____	_____
_____	_____	_____	_____
_____	_____	_____	_____
		Sub Total	_____
		Shipping	add 10% of cost
		TOTAL	_____

Please send your order and all correspondence to:
Crusaders Ministries
P.O. Box 7211
Chicago, Illinois 60680